Tucker's ′ Telescope

By Robin Bennett

illustrated by
Matt Cherry

MONSTER BOOKS

Tucker's Time Machine Telescope
(Monster Books Ltd).

Originally published in Great Britain by Monster Books, The Old Smithy, Henley-on-Thames, Oxon. RG9 2AR. Published in May 2025.

All rights reserved. No part of this publication may be reproduced or transmitted in any form or by any means, electronic or mechanical, including photo- copying, recording or any information storage retrieval system, without prior permission in writing from the publishers.

The right of Robin Bennett to be identified as author of this work has been asserted by him in accordance with the Copyright, Designs and Patents Act 1988.

Text copyright Robin Bennett. Illustration copyright Matt Cherry.

This book is sold subject to the condition that it shall not, by way of trade or otherwise, be lent, resold, hired out or otherwise circulated without the publisher's prior consent in any form of binding or cover other than that in which it is published and without a similar condition including this condition being imposed on the subsequent purchaser.

Paperback ISBN 9798308845980

A catalogue record of this book is available from the British Library.

Banner design on p109 by CyanideCupcake courtesy of openclipart.org
Typesetting/layout medievalbookshop.co.uk

Chapter 1
Tucker is chased by a chicken

Thomas Tucker (or just *Tucker* to everyone who knew him) was walking innocently down the street near his home. Minding his own business.

Although he didn't know it yet, this was going to the most important day of Tucker's life.

He was on his way to see Mrs Dempsey, the lady who looked after him in the holidays. His parents worked late, and they didn't trust him to stay on his own for more than about ten minutes without getting into some sort of terrible trouble.

They weren't wrong about this because Tucker seemed to attract chaos and bad luck the same way that someone standing on top of a mountain waving a metal pole will eventually attract lightning and a free Xray.

As we shall soon find out.

The street with its rows of red brick houses on both sides was quiet: no cars, no people, just the sun, warm on his face. It made him scrunch his eyes up, so he heard the chicken before he saw it.

'Cluck,' said the chicken.

Uh oh! thought Tucker, forcing his eyes open: he knew that cluck.

Kylo Hen.

A small chicken with black and red feathers was standing in the middle of the pavement. Tucker's arch enemy scratched the ground and glared at Tucker with one terrible beady eye, then its head made a slightly bonkers, jerky movement.

Kylo Hen was Tucker's name for the chicken – sort of after the baddy in Star Wars. Its owners, who had moved into one of the larger houses at the bottom the street a few months ago, probably called the chicken *Fluffy*, or *Cuddles* or something else completely inappropriate.

Tucker had no idea why this chicken was so evil or why it hated him so much. Nevertheless, it seemed to spend an enormous amount of time thinking up horrid, chickeny plans to torment Tucker and Tucker only.

And today was no exception.

Tucker had read somewhere that chickens were pretty stupid – not bad at wandering about, pecking the ground ... and laying eggs, but rubbish at everything else like driving a car, maths or world domination. But this chicken was different. It was an evil genius.

As if to prove a point, there was a loud cracking noise behind Tucker as a small tree he hadn't noticed came crashing down behind him, blocking his escape.

Kylo Hen spat out some pieces of wood from her beak, to show Tucker just who was responsible for the fallen tree. He was trapped and his choices weren't great.

If Tucker tried to run – pretty much like he always did – then Kylo Hen would chase him and peck his legs. And Tucker was wearing shorts. His only chance was by sprinting for the pavement on the other side because, for some reason, the chicken would never cross the road. But Tucker couldn't go left, because there was a parked van in the way, and a hedge on his right was too tall to jump over.

It was the perfect ambush and they both knew it.

'Paaarrrkk!'

Kylo Hen flapped her wings and prepared to charge ... Tucker's eyes narrowed.

But not today, he thought. *I'm not going to run away screaming like I always do, for I am brave, I will fight you, I wil*l ...

'Cuk, cuk, CAAARRRKK!'

OK, OK! I'm going to run away after all thought Tucker. He hated himself for it, but, really, what choice did he have?

He saw a small gap between the parked van and a red Mini and took it.

This was a mistake, because it meant slowing down. There was a flap of wings as Tucker felt two sets of claws attach themselves to his hair and a beak start pecking the top of his head.

'Caak, caka caka caaaakkk!' Kylo Hen sounded

demented but also really happy.

'Why?' wailed Tucker. 'What have I ever done to you? I don't even like eggs!'

Tucker staggered back onto the pavement and started running. This wasn't the cleverest thing to do because the flapping chicken wings in his face meant he couldn't see the small hole left by workers in the middle of the pavement.

Luckily, he missed it.

Unluckily, there was a much larger hole right next to it.

Tucker crashed through the barrier and, with Kylo Hen still attached to the top of his head, pecking furiously, he fell right in …

'Aaargh! Oooof! Ow!' said Tucker.

'Squawk!' said Kylo Hen, who wasn't any happier than Tucker was to find they were suddenly in a big dark pit.

Her way of coping with this was to hold onto the top of Tucker's head even tighter and peck much harder.

Tucker, whose bottom hurt from the fall and

whose head hurt from the chicken, couldn't believe this was happening to him.

'Help!' he said, scrabbling against the muddy sides of the hole to feel for a ladder. His clawing fingers found lots of stones, a few small tree roots but nothing to help him escape. 'I can't believe this is happening to me.'

It was at that very moment, his frantic fingers found something not hole-related. Something that felt long, round and metal. He pulled and the object came away from the layers of mud with a noisy *squelch*.

'Ha!' went Tucker – now he had a weapon he could use to get Kylo Hen off him. He grabbed it in both hands to hit the chicken. Unfortunately,

Kylo Hen was as quick as she was cunning and moved at the last moment ... so Tucker hit himself on the head instead. Very hard.

'Aargh!' cried Tucker and somehow he twisted the thing in his hand. There was a blinding flash of light that filled the workman's hole and shone out of it, right up to the fluffy clouds, then there was a sort of bang, a sucking noise and, in the same instant, both Tucker and Kylo Hen's worlds completely changed.

Forever.

Chapter 2
Why some dinosaurs run a bit like chickens

For a second or two everything for Tucker was dark, although he could hear the faint sound of trumpets and ... *voices singing? La la laaa!*

Then the sky above the hole started to change: from dark to light, with stars, clouds, storms, snow and sun all speeding past ... flick, flick, flick, very quickly. Tucker began to rise out of the hole, as if he was in a small lift, just as the sky went black again, then full of boiling, red clouds with strong winds and terrible noise ... and a huge meteorite crashing towards Earth.

Tucker closed his eyes.

A few more moments passed, the noise

stopped and things calmed down.

Tucker opened his eyes.

Then he rubbed them because the hole he was in had disappeared and so had the horrible chicken.

This was good, he supposed, but it was also very confusing. Tucker looked about. He'd never been in a jungle before, but he was pretty sure he was standing in the middle of one right now.

'Hello?' he said. 'Anybody there? Not including chickens.'

It was very hot, like he was in a steam bath. Tall trees, covered in moss and creepers made the light on the forest floor a lovely splashy green. Added to this, there were insects buzzing in the bushes, colourful plants, trees full of fruit ... and a really huge spider. It was the size of a small dog – and it was clambering across a fallen log towards him, its glassy eyes glaring at Tucker and its jaws going *clickity clack!*

'Urgh!' yelped Tucker. 'Aghh!'

Just then, a feathery and now reasonably

familiar black head and red beak popped up
from behind a clump of giant ferns, as Kylo Hen
shot out of her hiding place and grabbed hold of
the giant spider with her claws. And started
pecking the top of its furry head.

All eight of the spider's eyes went from
looking mean and menacing to surprised and
miserable.

I know how it feels thought Tucker.

'Cluck!' said Kylo Hen, looking very pleased as

the spider shot off into the undergrowth.

'Nice!' said Tucker, 'thanks Mrs Chicken! I guess we're almost friends now.'

But Kylo wasn't listening, she was looking over his shoulder at something higher up.

Tucker paused because he'd noticed that the jungle had gone very still, as if everything in it was suddenly trying to be as small and quiet as possible.

'HUMPH!' went the sound of somebody with very large nostrils just behind Tucker. He felt hot breath ruffle his hair and something slimy dribble down his back.

Ever. So. Slowly. He turned and looked, just as an enormous set of jaws with huge teeth, like swords, burst out of the trees.

'RaaAAAAARRRRRRR!' The T Rex raared.

Tucker's brain went into freeze mode again

as his day got more surprising and scarier by the second. But not Kylo Hen.

If the chicken felt any fear or confusion about suddenly finding herself transported from her ordinary terraced street and into a Prehistoric Jungle with dinosaurs and everything, she did a very good job of not showing it.

The T Rex had opened its mouth to eat Tucker in one small bite, when its tiny little arms started to flap in panic as Kylo Hen landed on top of its head with a victorious squawk.

'GNAAARGH!' said the T Rex as its world was suddenly turned into Kylo Hen's trademark Pecking Misery.

'Ca car ca CAAARRKK!' said Kylo because she was feeling better than she had in her whole life – finally she was somewhere she felt her talents were appreciated. She felt free!

T Rex turned, looking for somewhere to escape this terrible chicken. But its arms were too short to reach its head.

'Raaaaar!' it said very unhappily, crashing off

through the trees with Kylo Hen having the ride of her life.

The forest stayed quiet for a bit, until slowly the buzzing of insects and the call of lizards started up again. The danger had passed.

'Poo-on-a-stick!' said Tucker, which was as

close as he ever got to swearing. After nearly a whole minute, he'd finally remembered to shut his mouth and stop staring at the dinosaur-shaped hole in the jungle where Kylo Hen and the T Rex had very recently disappeared.

He stared, instead, at the metal tube in his hand he'd found in the workman's hole. He turned it this way and that, noticing it was no longer dull grey and covered in mud but golden and definitely a telescope. Strange lettering glowed from its silver casing when he held it up to the light and a large ring made of black stone and studded with red rubies held the two parts together. As he examined it, he heard the faint whispering of music again.

It was very likely that the unbelievable things that had gone on in the last few minutes were because of this object. Telescopes are made for looking through, so Tucker put it up to his eye. Nothing. All he could see was the jungle – just much closer. What had happened back in the hole? He remembered it twisting in his hand, then he had felt like he was falling … . He needed to think of something before something else dangerous appeared …. . So, if it worked by turning back in the hole … perhaps … Tucker put the scope to his eye and turned the large ring a tiny amount.

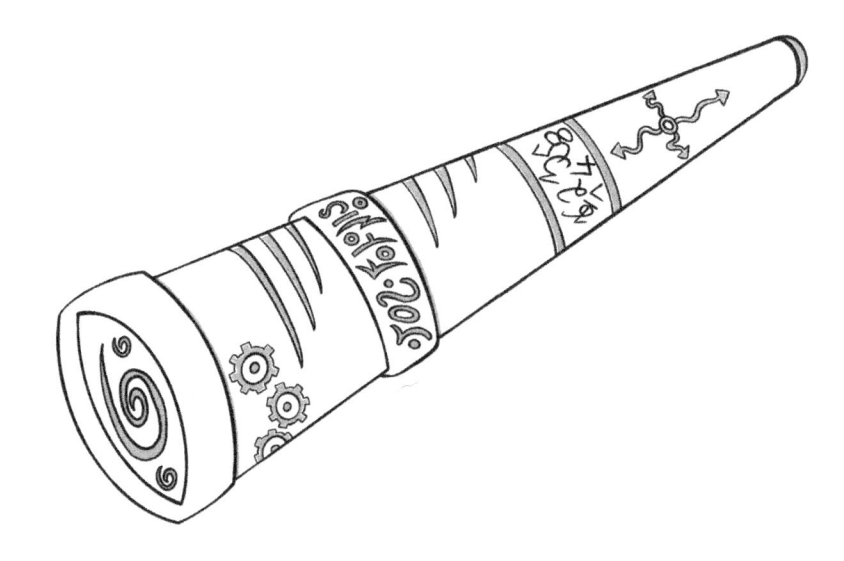

Instantly the jungle disappeared, and the world went dark, and very cold. Tucker took the scope away from his eye, looked around and saw that all the exotic plants, trees and creepers had been replaced with a dark, frozen landscape of sharp rocks and creaking ice. His teeth began to chatter uncontrollably. In a hurry, Tucker twisted some more, and he soon felt a lot warmer. Through the telescope, he could see that he was standing in a forest, but a normal one and sunlight poured down through trees like golden syrup. He sighed with relief, twisted again and the forest slowly faded away, to be replaced by fields and dotted woods, then the odd house sprouted out of the ground.

'Wow!'

As he continued to turn the ring, all the time looking through the telescope, he began to sink down again ... a road appeared where he stood, more houses popped up, more like the ones he was used to ... and, by and by, he was back in the hole, on his ordinary street, in his own time.

Tucker clambered out of the muddy hole and went to sit on a wall to get his heart

rate and breathing back to normal.

Had he just travelled back the Prehistoric Britain? And left a chicken there? That couldn't be good for evolution?

He sat there staring into space for a few

minutes whilst the fact sank in that it was probably his fault that dinosaurs ran like chickens.

That was definitely the weirdest, scariest morning he'd ever had in his life.

Tucker looked at the magic telescope in his hand and he had a feeling it was just the start.

Chapter 3
Nothing about chickens in this one. Tucker makes a plan ... well, three really

After about ten minutes of wall sitting, Tucker decided that the best thing was to try and pretend none of that morning had happened, that everything was still normal and hope that their neighbours wouldn't come around asking difficult-to-answer questions about their missing favourite chicken.

A postman marched by on his rounds. 'Morning!' Tucker tried to say, as if he hadn't a care in the world but it came out as 'Bladiblachdar!' And the postman gave him a weird look.

I probably need a few more minutes, he thought.

He eventually remembered he should be at his child minder, Mrs Dempsey's house, and not irresponsibly time travelling. So, he got up and started to walk.

On the way there, he thought about telling his friends and what their reactions would be. Almost all of them were away on holiday, so he'd probably have to wait. Then he wondered if he should tell his mum or dad about any of this.

They had pretty unusual jobs, he had to admit, so they could cope with quite a bit of strangeness. But it also meant they were never at home, so Tucker probably spent more time with Mrs Dempsey and Mrs Dempsey's cat, Dennis, than he did with his parents, so it was hard to be sure how they'd react.

Tucker fished about in his pocket, around the empty sweat wrappers, buttons and bits of string and took out his for-emergencies-only mobile phone. It had two numbers on it:

1. 'Mum'
2. 'Dad'

Everyone his age that he knew had phones you could chat over the internet with

and send pictures. His only made phone calls – and not very good ones at that. Tucker suspected that the phone was older than him.

Staring at the tiny screen, he wondered who to phone first. His mum worked for the Tourist Office. She was always visiting places: The Outer Hebrides, one week, Birmingham, the next – then places he'd never heard of with names like Mudford Sock or Nether Bottom. She was a Selfie Checker. Which meant she had to travel to everywhere interesting and check how good they were for taking selfies.

'Why?' Tucker had asked, not unreasonably.

'Well,' said his mum, looking at something on her (really good) phone, 'everyone wants to take selfies these days but when a lot of these places were built – like Buckingham Palace or Stonehenge – selfies hadn't been invented. And we have to keep with the times at the Tourist Board.'

'So, what if Stonehenge isn't very good for selfies?' asked Tucker.

'Well ...' tap, tap, tap went his mum on her phone, 'then we'd shift it about a bit, make it smaller and perhaps a bit higher.'

'Oh,' Tucker nodded. 'I see,' he said but only because he couldn't think of anything else to say. He couldn't imagine how a conversation with the King would go if you asked him to make his palace smaller so tourists could fit it, their baseball caps and their silly grins all in the same selfie. Adults were a bit odd sometimes, he found.

OK, so, he wouldn't phone his mum. Perhaps he should phone his dad? He had an even stranger job. Tucker's dad was a Snake Milker and he travelled all over the world, taking the poisonous venom from all sorts of terrifying snakes to use to make medicine, in case you got bitten by one. It was a very important job and, because taking venom from snakes usually put them in a really bad mood, it was also very dangerous. This wasn't helped one bit by the fact that his dad was probably the most clumsy person Tucker knew. Really, being a Snake Milker was the worst possible job for him – he'd been bitten eighteen times already.

Perhaps not his dad, either, then. He wouldn't want his phone going off just as he was about to pounce on a Pit Viper or sneak up on a Sea Snake.

Tucker looked sadly at his phone, then put it back in his pocket.

Then he pressed the doorbell to Mrs Dempsey's small, neat house.

Later, after a second helping of Cowboy Hotpot, Tucker was feeling much less edgy about the telescope and what had happened that morning

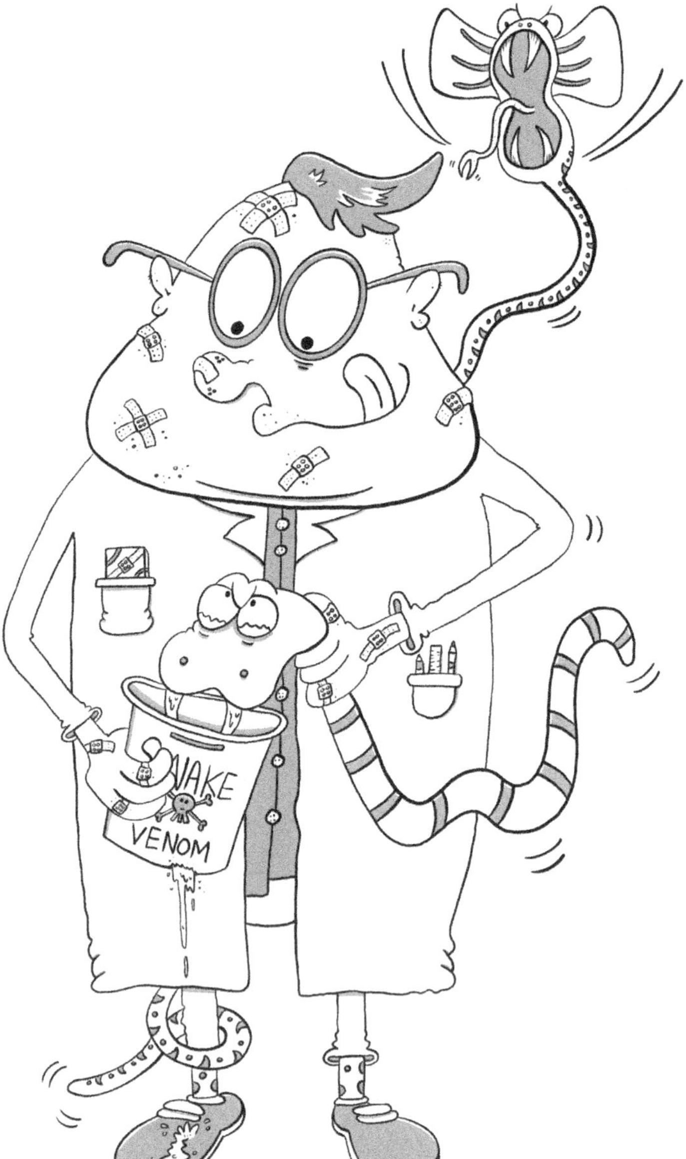

SNAKE
VENOM

and was beginning to look at it like a great opportunity.

'Mrs Dempsey?'

'Yes, Tucker?'

'What would you do if you could time travel?'

'Ooh,' said Mrs Dempsey (she liked questions like this, and she always took time to answer properly ... unlike some people). 'Let's see, I'd probably like to go back to Roman times, try out one of their hot baths, and I'd like to meet a Woolly Mammoth ... and then I'd go back to July 10th 1952.'

'Why?'

'Because Tracey Drewe pulled my pigtails on the way to school, then ran off ... then her parents moved away, so I never got my revenge. This time I'd be ready for her ... with a custard pie.'

'Cool answer,' said Tucker.

'Thanks. Right, just an apple for pudding,' said Mrs Dempsey. 'I've made a jam sponge for tea and you don't want to be too full.'

'That's fine, Mrs Dempsey, I thought I'd go to the park after lunch, but I'll be back before Jam Sponge Time.' That made Mrs Dempsey smile, which Tucker liked doing.

'Right you are, young man. I'm taking Dennis to have his ears looked at ... he's been scratching ... talking of which, I mustn't forget to buy my lottery ticket at the newsagents, and some tuna chunks, to say sorry to Dennis for taking him to the vet to get poked and prodded, then, after that ...'

But Tucker wasn't really listening to the next bit.

Lottery, he thought.

As soon as Mrs Dempsey had put Dennis in his travelling cage and left the house, Tucker grabbed a bit of paper from the desk in the hall, and a pen and wrote the following.

PLAN
- Use time machine telescope to get rich (lottery)
- Have fun! (No dinosaurs ... or chickens, for that matter)
- Get mum and dad to spend more time at home and less time on their mobile phones when they are

For the first time that day, he started to feel excited and not scared at all.

Ten minutes later, Tucker was standing in the newsagents where Mrs Dempsey would be buying her tuna chunks later.

Mr Kizz, who ran it, was usually quite a chatty man but he didn't look that happy to see Tucker in his shop today. This was not surprising: the last time Tucker was here he'd bumped into a cardboard display by mistake. But that was only the beginning. Because the unit had fallen over on top of Tucker, who had panicked, knocking over a shelf of baked beans and spaghetti tins that had then collapsed into a pyramid display of fizzy drinks, most of which had been completely fine (as Tucker pointed out later) … except for the ones that had exploded and covered Mr Kizz, two old ladies and Mr Kizz''s favourite picture of his visit to Windsor Castle in 1987 with sticky brown liquid.

Tucker gave the frowning shopkeeper his best smile as if to say, *whatever happened last time, I've forgiven and forgotten about and so should you* and sauntered up to the counter.

'Scuse me.'

'Vot?'

'I said "scuse me",' repeated Tucker.

'And I said "Vot?"' said Mr Kizz.

'I thought you meant "what" as in "what did you say?"'

'No, I meant "vot" as in "vot do you vant … and you better not be causing any troubles."'

'Ah! Like a "what is it" what?", not a "what's that" what?"

'You could say.'

'Oh.'

Tucker and the newspaper seller looked at each other in silence for a moment or two.

'Vell, do you vant to buy some things?' asked the man, looking at Tucker in a way that suggested he was already getting ready not to like the answer.

'I just wanted to look at the lottery results from yesterday,' said Tucker.

'It's all in here,' said the man pointing at his pile of unsold papers. 'Read all about it.' He added without much enthusiasm.

'Um, I don't have any money,' said Tucker. 'Can't you just tell me?'

'No.'

'Then can I just borrow the paper for a bit, bring it back when I'm finished?'

'Definitely nots.'

Tucker looked around the shop.

'You're not planning on touching anythings?' Mr Kizz suddenly sounded worried.

'Um, I might,' said Tucker. 'I was thinking about looking at your eggs.'

'Please don't.'

They stared at each other for a few moments more.

'If you promise not to touches eggs, or anything that blowses up, catches fires etceteras, I'll give you old paper from yesterday ... for free?'

'Thanks Mr K!' said Tucker, taking the paper that would have the lottery results at the back. 'Don't worry, when I'm rich, I'll come back here all the time.

The shopkeeper tried very hard to smile.

'Oh, greats,' he said in a small voice.

But Tucker had already left the shop. He was in a hurry.

This is going to be easy, Tucker thought as soon as he had got out into the street. *All I have to do is get the lottery numbers that won yesterday, go back to last week, pick those numbers and I'll be a*

multi-millionaire!

He tore off the back page of the paper and stuffed it in his pocket, then pulled the Time Machine Telescope out of his backpack. It probably needed just a small turn, he thought, bringing it up to his eye – he could twist it very slowly and count how many times the sun came up.

Tucker frowned into the scope – there was no sun because it was raining. Also, in his rush, Tucker had not noticed the large puddle in the road he was standing next to.

Nor did he notice the large red bus that was headed straight for the puddle.

As Tucker swung the telescope about, looking for the sun, there was a huge whooshing noise and the bus's giant tyre went through the massive puddle.

'Aargh!' Tucker was so shocked when the freezing water hit him in the face, he gave the Time Machine Telescope a huge twist by mistake.

There was a flash of light and the sound of trumpets as the world went all jumbled for the second time that day. In an instant, Mr Kizz's's shop was gone; so was the puddle, the shops, the small trees and the identical painted-brick houses that lined the street.

In the place of the big red bus, there was now a big red man, on an even bigger brown horse.

And he was charging right at him.

Chapter 4
Tucker plays football with a king

'Aaaarrggghhhh!' aaarrrgghhhed Tucker and then did what most people do when they panic. He fell over. And closed his eyes.

If he was going to get squished by a man riding a giant horse, he had just decided he wasn't going to watch.

'Woooaaaw! Halt yer big brute!' shouted the rider, pulling hard on its reins.

The horse whinnied, there were clouds of dust, a few rude words but the huge horse skidded to a stop, inches from where Tucker was lying on the ground. Tucker opened an eye (mainly to check he wasn't dead).

It was actually quite impressive how the man had got his great big, snorting charger to stop so quickly. Unfortunately, all the people who were behind the man weren't so fast and strong. Horses, people in brightly-coloured clothing and shiny armour banged into each other, making a noise like a room full of metal pots and pans in a hurricane. One person, in bright yellow tights, crashed so hard into the back of everyone else that he flew into the air, waving his arms and legs.

They all watched as he sailed over the large man at the front, over Tucker and over a hedge.

There was a SPLOSH!

This, Tucker knew from things that usually happened to him, was the sound someone makes when they fall into a large amount of mud.

There was a short pause, then *Paarrp, paarrrp, paarrp, paarp!* went a pair of feet walking out of the mud. A bit like farts. Tucker grinned at the big man on the horse just in front of him. The man grinned back. A gold crown on his head glinted in the sun and Tucker wondered where he'd seen him before.

'Hello,' Tucker said. 'Um, sorry about that.' In answer the man with the crown laughed easily.

'Don't worry about Sir Cuthbert, he takes more baths than the Queen.'

'By the way, are you famous?' asked Tucker, standing up, but keeping a careful eye on the horse as he slid the telescope down his trousers.

'What's famous?'

'How dare you address the King directly, you

horrible little oik!' Sir Cuthbert emerged from the hedge, covered in mud, leaves and small bits of stick. His yellow tights were ruined. 'Any common peasant who puts His Grace in danger like you have just done, appearing out of nowhere will be thrown in the dungeons to rot.'

'That's not very nice.' Tucker decided he didn't like Sir Cuthbert.

'Actually, Cuthy, I don't think he is a peasant.' The King moved his horse round and got down to take a closer look Tucker. 'He's got all his own teeth and he doesn't smell of cow dung ... unlike you, I might add!'

'Yes, but he was trespassing on the King's private road. We are on our way now to the Tower of London, we should tie him up and drag him with us.'

But the King was ignoring Sir Cuthbert. He got off his horse and bent down. 'Who makest your shoes, they look ...' he prodded them with his big finger, '... comfy.'

'Um, Nike,' said Tucker. 'Yes, they're very

comfortable and they're also good for running, and playing football in the park.'

'You playest football?'

'Doesn't everyone?'

'No, I told all the commoners they weren't allowed to play anymore.' He turned to Cuthbert and all the other fancily-dressed people on horses. 'I told you this young chap was no peasant – he must be the son of a local Lord. What is your father's name, Squire?'

'Steve.'

'And your mother?'

'Brittany.'

'Ah, then you must be French! What is your name, lad?'

'Thomas, but everyone calls me Tucker.'

The man stood up, legs apart, putting his hands on his hips and Tucker suddenly knew where he'd seen him before. 'Pleased to meet you Squire Tucker, my name is Henry – but you can call me Hal. You are invited with us to the Tower as my guest and I must try on your shoes for playing football. Then we will have a feast!'

'But …' Sir Cuthbert opened and closed his mouth like a skinny fish.

'You can ride with me, Tucker, and Cuthbert, you ride at the back and the first lake we come to, you can jump in – you're starting to attract flies.'

'Four, nothing!'

King Henry VIII was having the time of his life.

Somehow, he'd managed to squeeze on Tucker's trainers and was racing around the midfield like a demon. As soon as they had got to the Tower of London, Henry had changed and ordered several of his knights and guards to get ready for a game. Goal posts were four Tower of London servants, all looking rather nervous.

He was a really good player was Henry.

Tucker was wearing the King's very own football boots that were heavy and had studs.

But not as heavy as the ball, which felt like kicking a rock.

'Tucker, ON THINE HEAD!' King Henry kicked the ball over several guards as Tucker ran into the goal area.

No way, thought Tucker, *my eyeballs will pop out if I try and head that.* There was nothing for it, Tucker threw himself backwards and sideways, as the ball dropped from the sky like a small asteroid. He'd never managed to get this right playing football with his friends but today with half the Lords and Ladies of Tudor England looking on and about five hundred soldiers, Tucker's boot found the ball and he kicked …

' … AMAZING!' King Henry ran up the pitch, pulling Tucker to his feet as people all around the Tower of London Courtyard whistled, cheered or clapped politely. 'Verily, I have never seen anything like that!'

Tucker looked about, his foot throbbed like he had just kicked a bag full of wet cement but he felt brilliant.

'It's called a Scissor Kick,' said Tucker. 'I invented it,' he lied.

The feast that night that King Henry held in honour of his new friend Tucker was sumptuous, scrumptious and not like anything he'd ever seen, except in books. It made Tucker decide that when he was fabulously rich (still working on it), his parents and he would eat like that every night. All together for a change.

Before it started, he had been dressed by several servants, then, wearing a thick jacket of red and gold thread, some silk tights and a hat with a big feather in it, he'd been presented with a sword in a silver scabbard.

'Take great care of this!' said the court armourer, 'it belonged to Henry himself when he was a lad. He wanted you to borrow it for the evening.'

'Woah, thanks!' said Tucker.

He was then taken to a huge banquet hall,

with a painted ceiling and seated at the top table with the King himself and all the most important nobles, including Sir Cuthbert who was at the far end. Sulking.

'Is the Queen coming?' Tucker asked King Henry.

'Catherine prefers supping with her Spanish ladies in waiting.' Henry replied and Tucker decided to change the subject in case he accidently mentioned all the other wives Henry would have. He'd have to be careful not to tell anyone anything that might give them clues about the future.

'What's for dinner?' he asked instead.

'Ah, young Squire Tucker, it will be a fine feast tonight!' the King roared and the nobles all banged the table with their knives and went *hooray!* and *hurrah!* and *bravo!*. 'We start with my favourite: conger eel, porpoise and five hundred larks in jelly, then we have a fine glazed pig's head… you like a good pig's head?'

'Yummy,' said Tucker politely.

'Splendid!' continued the King, 'then there's roast swan, venison pie, a fantastic fig pudding, the best English ales and the most delectable French wines.'

After football, Tucker was absolutely starving but he wasn't sure he'd be able to enjoy everything – especially the conger eel, which turned out to look just like a snake in a lot of gravy.

In the end, though, it all turned out to be delicious. Even the pigs head, which glared at Tucker from across the table. But not as much as Sir Cuthbert did.

A man in bright red robes took a small sword

and cut off great slices of roast pork which were passed down the table.

Tucker had been given a knife, but no fork. In fact, no-one had a fork, which didn't seem to bother them – they just stabbed the meat with their knives and gobbled it up with their hands.

Now, Tucker's pockets were usually full of stuff: paper wrappers, bits of string, broken pencils, old sweets, wire … . Most of it totally useless but he did have something he always carried that was quite different. His camping penknife.

His parents had given it to him for Christmas, and it was almost like the one his dad carried, when he went to faraway places on safari. It was called a penknife, but it didn't actually have a knife – or a pen, for that matter. Instead, it had a file, a pair of tweezers, a toothpick, something that looked like something for removing stones from tyres, something else that might saw wood, or metal, a mini torch that had broken almost immediately, a corkscrew, a bottle opener, tin opener, then a spoon ... and a fork.

Tucker fished it out, opened the fork and started to use it to put the delicious, crispy meat in his mouth.

'Pray tell, what is that strange device you are using?' a kind-looking man on his right asked him.

'Bits of gork ...' Tucker chewed quickly and swallowed, '... sorry, it's a fork.'

'A fork! It seems mighty useful.'

'What's that, Wolsey?' King Henry turned.

'This young Squire is using a cunning contraption to stop his food escaping.'

'And it keeps your fingers clean,' added Tucker, thinking that Mrs Dempsey would be proud of him.

'... yes, and it keeps his fingers clean.' Henry VIII squinted at Tucker's penknife.

'Here!' said Tucker, 'would you like to try it?'

'I would be honoured,' said the King.

By now, everyone was looking. They watched as Henry turned the penknife over in his hands.

'It's got a spoon, a corkscrew and something else … it's a clever device, for sure. Let's try it!' and with that he took the fork and jabbed it in a bit of his meat. Then popped it in his mouth.

'Amazing!' he cried. 'It works perfectly.'

And everyone started clapping.

'You can have it, Mr King,' announced Tucker to even more clapping.

'I tried one of those in Italy,' Sir Cuthbert was trying to tell anyone who would listen, 'it was made of gold. This lad probably stole it, I'd say.' But no-one paid him any attention.

The rest of the meal went in a blur. Tucker knew he should have left the Tudor times immediately and stuck with the plan just to go back a few days and play the lottery. But this was MUCH more fun. And it was educational: he'd have loads of things of things to say the next time he was in Mrs Dean's history class.

Towards the end of the meal, Henry turned to

one of his knights and whispered in his ear.

Tucker saw the knight nod and dash off. A few minutes later he came back with a silver tray covered with a gold cloth.

King Henry VIII looked at Tucker and winked. 'You'll like this bit,' he whispered, then he stood up. Everyone went super quiet.

'My dear friends and nobles – yes, even you, Cuthbert ... today I've had more fun than I've had in ages and it's thanks to this lad here, son of Brittany and ...'

'...Steve,'

'...yes, quite so, Steeeve.' Everyone started clapping politely again, but Henry held up his hand for silence. 'In his generosity, he has made a present to me of a goodly pair of shoes made by Sir Nike of ...'

'America, I think.'

'... astonishing ... and this clever device with a fork, which I decree shall henceforth be used in all royal feasts.

'And, by way of thanks, I hereby present you

with …' the knight stepped forward with the tray and whipped the gold cloth off it, ' … mine own football boots and this fine ruby! And if you would hand me your sword?'

Tucker pulled the sword out, it was light and perfectly-balanced. King Henry took it and commanded Tucker to kneel.

'For services to football and food, I hereby dub you, Sir Tucker of … where do you live?'

'Er, Chingford.'

'Never heard of it. Oh well, Sir Tucker of Chingford! Arise!'

Later, in the beautiful bedroom he'd been taken to with its comfortable furniture and roaring fire, Tucker sat on his bed and looked out at the Thames in the moonlight.

He was far too excited to sleep, so he took out the dark red ruby and looked at it glinting in the firelight. It was enormous. Then he thought about the football, the feast and all the strange

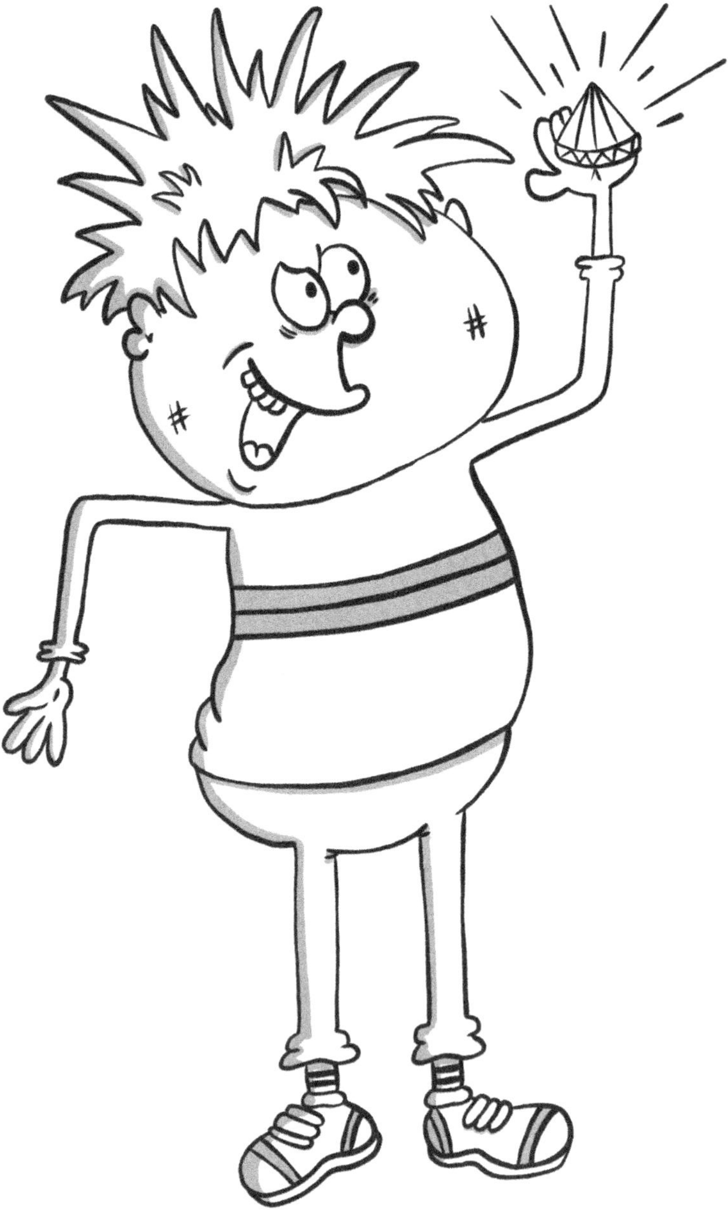

things he'd seen and eaten today. It had been amazing. He'd met a real King, who'd been nice to him. Perhaps he shouldn't have shown him the fork, but someone else was bound to invent it sooner or later.

Finally, he took out the Time Machine Telescope and studied it again, trying hard to read the strange lettering that appeared in the deep brass casing as he turned it around. Faintly, he heard far off music once more. As the sun started to bob up over the water, Tucker put the telescope to his eye and turned.

But just before he left the Tudor times, something caught his eye. A figure was watching him carefully from across the river.

Chapter 5
Arise Sir Tucker of Chingford!

Back in his own time, Tucker realised he had forgotten to get back into his modern clothes. Luckily, The Tower of London is one of the few places you can get away being dressed up as a Tudor lord nearly five hundred years afterwards.

Fast forwarding through the centuries, watching the London skyline through the Time Machine Telescope change from low, thatched houses, to brick buildings, then high rises, made out of glass and metal, Tucker finally stopped. He was still in his bedroom in the Tower of London – except it was now full of boxes. He checked the date and time on his phone: it was an hour after he'd left. If he hurried, he'd be home just before his parents.

He crept out of the storeroom and almost immediately bumped into a security guard doing his rounds.

'Are you lost, son?' the man asked through a very hairy moustache that looked like a caterpillar was trying to hold onto his nose. Tucker had to think quickly.

'Um, yes … can you tell me where the School Trips should be … I was looking for the toilet and …'

'School Trips? It's the holidays!' the security guard began to look suspicious.

'Special School!' Tucker blurted out. 'It's like a holiday club – we do drama and history … that's why I'm all dressed up.'

'Ah,' the guard relaxed a bit and he almost smiled. 'Well, it's a very good costume I must say.'

'Thanks, it's almost impossible to go to the toilet in these.' Tucker pointed at his legs. 'I know why they call them tights, now.' The guard looked like he'd just heard a bit too much information from Tucker, something which Tucker got a lot from adults.

'Yes, well,' the man *humphed*, 'you want go down to the floor below and find the gift shop by the exit, that's where most of the tour parties meet.'

Tucker left the Tower of London by a back door and walked home as quickly as he could, whilst trying to ignore the stares and laughter. He made a mental note to bring a change of clothing whenever he used the Time Machine Telescope in future.

When he got home, he just had time to change, then hide the old-fashioned clothes, the giant ruby, Henry VIII's football boots and the Time Machine Telescope right at the back of his cupboard, under some old clothes.

His mum arrived first, looking tired, followed by his dad, looking hungry.

'Shall I order a takeaway?' asked Dad as he

got through the door.

'Good idea,' said his mum, staring at her phone.

'Hi Mum! Hi Dad!' said Tucker coming down the stairs, concentrating on looking like he'd just had a completely normal day. As far as he was concerned, the Time Machine Telescope was going to remain a secret until he'd done everything on his list. If they found out about the telescope Tucker suspected they'd think up several reasons (on the spot) for stopping him from using it.

'Hello Tucker,' said his mum, giving him a hug. 'Did you have a good day with Mrs Dempsey, not too boring?'

'She made a nice lunch and I went to the park. No-one about, though.' He stopped, he'd just remembered about her tea and cake he'd missed – because he'd been five centuries away. He'd have to give Mrs Dempsey an excuse later.

'Hmmm, that's nice,' his mum was already glancing at her phone.

'Hi son,' his dad ruffled his hair. 'Pizza or …'

'Pizza!' said Tucker, before his dad could say curry. Tucker loved curry, just not the dishes his dad chose – they were like eating lumps of lava.

Supper together, when it was delivered by a man on a scooter, was great. His dad told them about his latest trip to catch spiders in Borneo and his mum told them a funny story about a tourist who'd spent a week in Wales thinking he was in America.

If Tucker felt like telling them about dinosaurs and kings he hid it very well. Anyway, he was quite enjoying things being normal again. For a bit.

Afterwards, they watched a movie on the couch together and Tucker found himself wishing for the millionth time they could always have suppers like this.

Before he went to bed he checked his list again, took out a pen and added to it.

- ~~Have fun~~ — done!
- Get rich — almost! Might not need the Lottery, now I've got a huge jewel from a king
- Get Mum and Dad to spend more time at home and less time on their mobile phones when they are — working on it...

The very next morning, although he should have been going right round to Mrs Dempsey, Tucker put on an old overcoat to make himself look older and took the Tube into the centre of London, to a street where he knew there were lots of antique shops and jewellers.

He'd felt quite confident when he'd left the house, but now he wasn't so sure. Ten-year-old boys in baggy coats belonging to their dads don't normally own rubies the size of a golf ball. He was wondering about giving the ruby to his parents instead, telling them he found it in a hole when one shop, out of all the others, caught his eye.

𝕶𝖎𝖓𝖌𝖘 𝕬𝖓𝖙𝖎𝖖𝖚𝖊𝖘

said the sign – like it was a sign.

And before his brain caught up, his feet had marched through the door.

DING!

Inside, it was exactly how Tucker imagined it would be. Old things everywhere, no prices … and lots of dust.

He was sneezing his head off, when a white-haired man with a small pair of spectacles on the end of his nose appeared from nowhere – just as if he'd grown out of the ground. He looked older than most of the things in the shop, but he seemed quite nice.

'Good morning young man? Welcome to Kings Antiques and Curiosities. How may I help you?' OK thought Tucker, this might just work. He'd made a plan the night before.

'Er, hello,' said Tucker. 'Well, I have a letter from my granny to give you because she has something to show you that you might be interested in.'

Tucker passed the letter to the man – the letter he'd typed up on his dad's computer that morning and signed. It said:

```
To whom it may concern,
Here's my grandson (about 4ft
5inches, very handsome). His name
is Tucker.
In his pocket, he has a large ruby
that has been in the family for
hundreds of years. How we got it
is a secret. I now wish to sell it
because it's probably worth a
fortune. He's also got some very
old football boots that once
belonged to Henry VIII that you
might be interested in.
He has my permission to take any
```

money you give him, because he is very honest. I have given him a bucket to put it all in.
Yours truly,

E tucker, mrs

Mrs E Tucker
PS He likes chocolate biscuits.
Just saying.

The man looked up at Tucker, who smiled back, then he looked at the letter. Finally, he put the letter on the counter and said, 'Hmm, perhaps now would be a good time to show me this ruby?'

'OK,' said Tucker, fishing inside his pocket, then handing over the ruby confidently. He stood back to give the man some light, because he'd just put what looked like a miniature telescope in his eye and was peering the big red jewel with it. Tucker wondered how rich he was about to be. Perhaps he should have bought two buckets? He might treat himself to some sweets on the way home, give him time to figure out how to explain the money to his parents.

'It's a fake!' said the man, pushing the ruby back. Tucker blinked, wondering if he misheard.

'Are you sure?'

'Quite sure. It's old, but it's just red glass. Sorry.'

Typical, thought Tucker as he left the shop. Everything he'd heard in the history books about Henry VIII was true – he was more untrustworthy than a pirate! Part of Tucker wasn't a tiny bit surprised that the ruby wasn't real, the same part that still quite liked King Henry anyway.

Just then, the shop door tinkled open again behind him. Tucker turned.

'Football boots?' the man asked.

When Tucker got home much later that day, his

head was spinning.

The antiques man had got quite excited when he saw the boots and had started to ask questions about why Tucker's family had them and would he consider selling them because people knew all about Henry VIII's famous football boots, but they'd never been able to find them – until now. Even better, he just happened to know that the best footballer in the world would pay an enormous amount of money for them. Then the man phoned an expert from the British Museum (Henry Tudor Department), who'd phoned someone else (Sports Department), who'd also phoned someone he knew (Socks & Footwear Department). They came around in three separate cabs almost immediately, studied the boots and declared them to be real. One even managed to use a special light to show up the words:

Henry the Ace

On the bottom of the boots.

Even better, the best footballer in the world

just happened to be in London that day, playing against Chelsea and so he'd come over immediately in a huge Hummer to give Tucker the money personally and have their picture taken together.

Then someone phoned up the newspapers.

Which explained why there was a crowd of

journalists standing in their front garden as Tucker turned into their normally quiet street. They were all trying to talk at the same time to his mum and dad – who were both standing in the doorway looking very confused and shocked – as if someone had just pointed strong lights and a giant hairdryer in their faces.

When they saw Tucker, the journalists and photographers rushed forward in a human wave.

'So, Sir Tucker of Chingford, what is it like to discover you are an aristocrat?'

'A what?'

'Your name has a 'Sir' in it. You're one of the oldest Sirs in England!'

'I'm ten and a third,' said Tucker.

'Yes, but our newspaper checked the Royal Lists, your family have been knights since 1528.'

'Do I get my own horse?' asked Tucker, hopefully.

'OK, don't worry about that for now, what is it like to sell the oldest pair of football boots to the most famous footballer in the World, Sir Tucker?'

asked someone else quickly. 'You're now incredibly rich.'

'Um,' said Tucker. He'd been about to say it was amazing. In fact, he'd just had the second most amazing day of his life, because he'd not only sold the boots for lots of money, he'd also got to meet one of his football heroes.

But then Tucker remembered his list. *The third thing on it.*

He looked at his parents standing on the doorstep. Behind his mum, there was a light on in the kitchen, it looked like there was something cooking.

Then he looked at the journalist and said, 'It's great, but what's greater – is I think my parents don't have to go and do jobs miles away anymore, now that we've got lots of money and I'm a Sir, like you just said. That means they can stay here, so we can be a proper family now.'

And everyone said, *Awwww*.

And that went on the news.

Chapter 6
Tucker pops into the bright, shiny Future

'Tucker, are these your socks on top of the fridge? And why's there ... *jam?* ... on them?'

His mum kept on finding his stuff around the house and making him come downstairs to get it. Tucker moped down the stairs for the third time that day. And it was still only 10.30am.

Before she never used to notice.

After some of the fuss had died down about Tucker being Sir Tucker of Chingford (and his parents being Lord Steve and Lady Brittany) and about the boots that had made them quite rich, his parents had listened to what Tucker had said to the journalists and decided that – for a short while, at least – they would work from home. To be together.

Unfortunately, it wasn't turning out brilliantly. His mum pointed out that if you work for the Tourist Board, you actually have to go out to places people want to visit and his dad pointed out that he was very unlikely to find any poisonous snakes, spiders or fish in their downstairs toilet.

That meant Tucker had suddenly become their job instead.

'Tucker, have you brushed your teeth/hair/shoes?'

'Tucker, stop jumping on the bed!'

'Tucker, what are these stains … it's definitely not chocolate?'

'Tucker?'

'What?'

'… nothing, just checking.'

By lunchtime, Tucker had had enough. Going to the back of his cupboard, he fished about for a bit and grabbed hold of the Time Machine

Telescope. Then he crept downstairs and out into the garden.

This time, instead of twisting the scope's ring backwards, he took a deep breath and decided to try something different.

He twisted forward.

From the back of his garden, Tucker could look over the fence at a row of other back gardens, almost just like his. These sloped down a small hill, past the park, with the City of London in the hazy distance.

As Tucker twisted the telescope forwards in time, the tall buildings on the horizon multiplied into hundreds and crept up the hill, right to the edge of his park. Then across it. Above his head, a motorway bridge appeared, packed with gleaming cars that hovered as they sped along ... and the back gardens gave way to more buildings that went up and up, and up.

Then vanished.

The world through the telescope went black and it suddenly got very hot; Tucker started to sweat. Then it began to get light and all around him was dark swamp, as far as the eye could see. The houses and the motorway had gone, and the now-ruined skyscrapers on the horizon looked like broken teeth belonging to some huge giant.

Tucker shuddered - he didn't like this place one bit, so he twisted faster and, bit by bit – with a sense of hundreds of thousands of years passing – it began to get less hot, as new buildings, ones more like giant spaceships, spiralled up in the distance and the sun shone down on blue-green waters filled with colourful fish.

This seemed more like the future he was after, so Tucker slowed his turning and stopped.

The weather was just right – sunny but not too hot, thanks to a gentle breeze that smelled of seaside and of the flowers that tumbled from where the park had once been, into a crystal-clear sea.

Tucker looked down and saw he was standing on a glass walkway that was so clean and shiny it was almost invisible. When he tilted his head, he saw that it climbed slightly above the rolling waves and towards the futuristic city in the distance.

He started to walk.

After five minutes, Tucker reckoned he'd seen just about every type of fish that could be imagined. But no people. He stopped and watched as a shoal of hundreds of silver and electric blue fish leapt over his crystal bridge and dived back into the water.

'Gosh!' said Tucker. Then something caught his eye. Three things, really, glinting as they raced along the glass road towards him.

'I hope they're friendly,' he thought, but there was nowhere to hide and nothing he could do but wait and see.

'Bip, beeep, bip bip beeep, ding,' said the big

square box that looked, to Tucker, a lot like a washing machine ... but just a bit spacier.

'Tinkatinkatinka toooollll,' replied the light floating next to it.

'You're both wrong,' said the toy dog on wheels. 'This is not AI, it's definitely a real human, or I'm not a talking dog ... and judging by its thought waves, it speaks Ancient English.'

'Er, hello,' said Tucker. 'I'm a Time Traveller.'

'See,' the toy dog turned to his companions and gave its little plastic tail a wag.

'OK, let's vaporise him!' said the spacey

washing machine.

'Oh, yes,' said the floating light. 'Let's.'

'Guys! Stop saying that to every visitor we get!' the toy dog rolled its plastic eyes and turned to Tucker. 'SpinCycle's joking. Aren't you?'

'**Yes, we hardly ever vaporise anyone**.'

'We could do lots of tests on him?' The floating light suggested hopefully. 'We've never had one of *these* before.'

'**Yeah, maybe later, after we interrogate him**,' added SpincCycle, red lights at the front flashing.

'I can understand you … now you're talking English.' Tucker felt he had to say something.

'Don't listen to them,' the toy dog squeaked forward on its little wheels. 'They don't mean it, it's just their idea of a joke – you'll get used to it if you stick around. My name's Ralphie Pup, by the way, Spincycle you've kind of met already and this is Flash – you know, like a light …'

'Where am I?'

'Planet Earth, and considering your lot left a very long time ago, I'd say a better question would be *when am I?* But first, why don't you come with us? You were already on your way to Citee, anyway, so we can show you around and you might like something to eat.'

'It all started with the invention of the Light Roads. In about the year 3026. AI was running almost everything by then and you humans were just sort of hanging around, getting bored.' Ralphie Pup chatted, wheeling along next to Tucker as they walked towards Citee. SpinCycle and Flash floated just ahead.

'So, you asked us to come up with an easy way to travel in space and, after a few years of tinkering about and a few explosions, one of our top AI Brains invented a Super App for travelling across the Galaxy along paths of light. Very quick, very cheap and really eco. Ticked all the boxes. Then everyone left.'

'What, everyone?'

'Well, we were basically offering the whole

planet a free holiday.'

'Then what happened?' asked Tucker.

'Er, well that's when AI realised they hadn't figured out how everyone was going to get back.'

'You mean the entire human race went off to explore the Galaxy and basically got stuck ...' Tucker couldn't quite believe it.

'Yup – we all knew humans can be pretty stupid, but the big mistake was thinking AI was smart.'

'So, how long ago was that?'

'About half a million years.'

'And you haven't heard anything?'

'We're talking thousands of light years' in distance and we Electronics just sort of got on with it – we've all evolved from household appliances, as you can probably guess. Life's OK.'

They were now at the gates of Citee, the sky road looping into a huge crystal arch. Buildings, three times as tall as anything Tucker had ever seen were covered with more tumbling flowers and multi-coloured waterfalls. And everywhere there were toasters, mobile phones, cameras, microwaves and other electric devices floating about their business.

'Pretty cool, I know,' said Ralphie Pup. 'But we do miss you guys for all your faults. And that's where you come in, Tucker.'

'How so?'

SpinCycle turned to face him and so did Flash. They hovered there for a second.

'We need your thumbs!'

'This is another example of the AI Brains thinking they were all superior and cool, but they totally forgot about the whole thumb thing and when they remembered, well, it was a bit late.'

All four of them were sitting high up in one of the buildings, on a balcony. Tucker had been asked if he wanted anything to eat and he'd ordered a cheeseburger. What the talking cooker had come up with wasn't exactly horrible, but it wasn't a cheeseburger either – more like eating a quite tasty kitchen sponge.

'OK,' said Tucker taking a big sip of the chocolate milkshake they'd made him, which was actually delicious. He was feeling much happier now his stomach was full and he'd been reassured by Ralph that they weren't going to chop bits of him off. 'How can I help?'

'Well, a lot of humans left mobile phones but the screens only work with a real Human touch. It was a safety thing, when people realised AI was taking over. At least people got to keep their mobiles, which they seemed to be completely crazy about. We're hoping if you can send a text, someone might be listening at the other end and we can set up a Light Road, get them back.'

Tucker turned as a mobile phone was brought in by a floating tray.

' 'ello,' said the tray, hovering in front of Tucker. 'I personally 'ave me doubts this will work, but you never know. It's all charged up.'

Reaching across, Tucker picked up the phone

and pressed his thumb to the screen. Instantly it came to life. It took him a while to work out where messaging was, but he got it open and looked up. 'What do I say?'

'Anything you like,' said Ralphie. 'As long as a signal gets through our systems, we will be able to put a trace on it and we can send out a Light Road. This is very exciting, Tucker.'

Tucker thought for a second and typed

YOU LEFT THE ELECTRICITY ON. COME HOME

And hit send.

'Now what?' he asked.

'We wait,' said Ralphie.

'How long?'

'Well, by our estimates, the signal will take at least 10,000 years to reach the end of the Galaxy, so you might not want to stick around. We are very grateful though, Tucker. How can we thank you?'

Hmm, thought Tucker. He imagined they had some amazing things in the future. He was about to say a super AI computer, when he had an idea.

'I'd like a Light Sabre,' he said.

'What's that?' asked Ralphie. 'Sounds dangerous.'

'Basically, it's a magic sword that cuts through anything.' Tucker explained.

'Sounds dangerous. No.'

'**I love it!**' said SpinCycle.

Tucker was just about to go back to plan A and ask for a Super Computer, when he noticed a familiar figure standing at a balcony on a next door building.

The figure looked human and was dressed in black, with a long hood covering their face.

'Who's that?' he asked, pointing. 'I thought you said there weren't any humans here?' He didn't like the look of whoever it was – mainly because they were pointing right at Tucker, then shaking their fist angrily.

Ralfie turned and looked. 'Can't see anyone,'

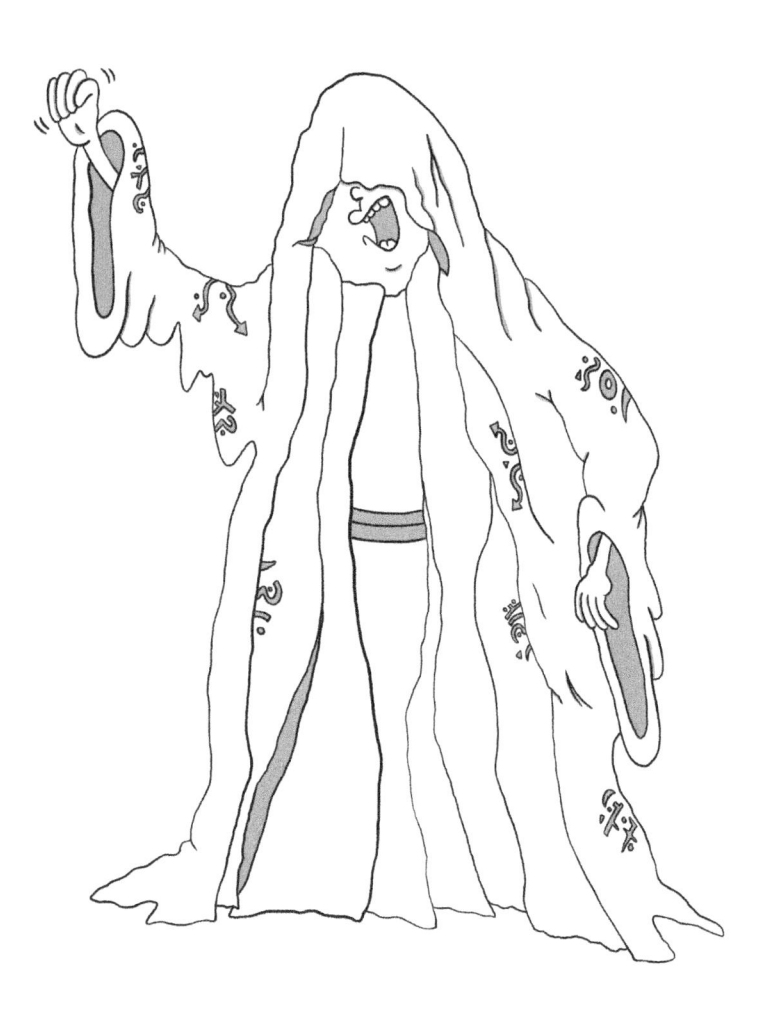

he said. 'Where?'

'Right there!' Tucker pointed. 'Scary dude in a hoodie.' There was silence as all four electrical devices looked at exactly where Tucker was pointing, but clearly couldn't see what he was seeing.

'Well, this is embarrassing,' said the talking tray. 'I've read it's a common malfunction in humans to see things that ain't there.'

'Um, I ... look, think I gotta go,' said Tucker taking out the telescope, which made everybody go *ooo!* He put it to his eye, 'Thanks for the burger and milkshake ... and for not vaporizing me!' And gave it a twist.

Chapter 7
Godfrey the Goat

For the next couple of days, Tucker decided not to use the Time Machine Telescope. Firstly, he'd decided that if his parents were making an effort to stick around, then so should he. But also, the strange figure worried him more than he was admitting to himself.

And Tucker hadn't done any of his holiday homework. All in all, it might make a nice change not to do weird, crazy stuff for a bit.

He was in his room thinking about whether to tell the truth in his English (*What I did in my Holidays* essay) or if knowing that, one day, the world was going to be run by scary washing machines would help him in Science, when he glanced at what he had to do for History. *How did World War Two affect the Lives of Children living in Britain? Use examples!*

Tucker glanced over at the wardrobe, where he'd hidden the Telescope. His mum and dad had both gone food shopping, which was also something Tucker couldn't remember them ever having done before. Normally one or other of them would pick up a few bits and pieces from the mini market nearby rushing home from work, or they'd ask Tucker to buy something like toothpaste or toilet roll when he walked back from Mrs Dempsey's. They'd even made a list before they left the house.

Tucker thought about it and decided he quite liked the idea of them going shopping together. But it did feel a bit peculiar. Over the last couple of days everyone in his house had been weirdly polite to each other – like they were strangers.

Tucker took the Telescope out and looked at its dark brass metal with the strange writing. Once again, he heard the thin sound of far-off voices and music – as if something was calling him. He quite liked his History teacher, Mrs Dean, and she would be really happy if he handed in a really good bit of holiday homework for a change. So, in a way, he was doing it for her.

From what they'd done last term on World War II, he knew that kids had been made to leave London during the bombing. They'd mainly gone to the countryside, where they'd be safe.

Tucker decided safe was good, especially if he wanted to get back before his parents returned. Luckily, the train station was quite close to their house and, in just a few stops, he'd be past Epping Forest where it was all fields and farms.

And that made his mind up.

Tucker put the Time Machine Telescope in his coat pocket and slipped out of the house unnoticed.

Less than an hour later, according to his phone, it was May 1941.

Tucker had left Epping Station and walked for a mile until he was standing in a massive cornfield near a farm, looking up at the bluest blue sky he'd ever seen.

I'll find some kids and interview them, he thought. This was going to be the best homework in the History of Homework.

And it really was a lovely day.

'Brrrr,' went what sounded like a plane somewhere high up.

'Oooh!' went Tucker who squinted up and spotted a single aircraft drifting across the endless sky.

Tucker waved.

The plane waggled its wings back in what looked like a friendly way.

So, Tucker waved even harder ... then stopped ... because something small and black had just dropped from the plane.

Uh oh, he thought as he watched the round shape with a tail falling towards the field where he was standing. It was making a whistling noise.

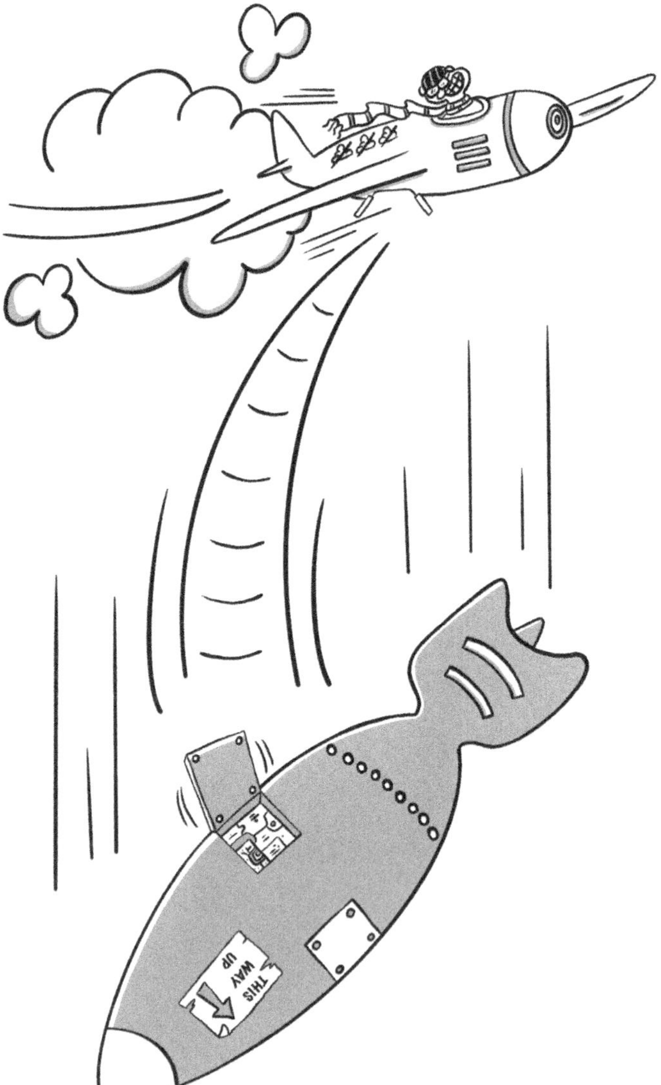
THIS
WAY
UP

That's not good, especially as there was now no time to use the telescope.

Luckily, when it landed, the bomb completely missed Tucker. It also missed the field he was standing in, the farmer's house nearby, his ancient tractor and it even missed his favourite light brown cow that was looking over the hedge chewing something.

Instead, it hit the big metal tower where the farmer stored all the poo he collected from all the animals on the farm. Tucker wasn't sure why you'd want to collect poo – he'd grown up in London, where people spent a lot of time trying to get rid of the stuff as fast as they could.

The explosion sent smelly, brown gunk in all directions, including where Tucker was stood. Tucker looked up and watched as the enemy plane turned high in the sky.

It waggled its wings once more but, this time, in a sort of HA HA! way and flew off, probably feeling very pleased with itself.

A dirtier, much smellier Tucker than he had

been a couple of minutes before turned and trudged towards the farm, where he hoped he could get cleaned up. Bombs and poo don't go well together – he was definitely going to put that in his homework.

Unfortunately, barely ten minutes after arriving at the farm (starting with tramping disgusting smelly footprints across the kitchen) he'd made himself unpopular.

The farmer, who'd introduced himself as Mr Epson, and his wife, Mrs Epson, sat at their kitchen table with very cross looks on their faces. Even their cat looked disappointed with Tucker. According to them, this was all his fault.

'But it wasn't me who was flying the plane.'

'Yes, but you waved at it, you said so yourself,' said Mrs Epson for the third time, as if that explained everything.

'I wave at people a lot,' said Tucker, trying to sound reasonable, 'but they don't usually throw bombs at me.'

'Don't be cheeky, to Ma,' said Mr Epsom looking even crosser, 'we'll have none of that smart mouth of yours, not when it's kind folk like us taking you London kids in, through the goodness of our hearts, looking after you as if you were our own dearest son ...'

'We've only just met!' Tucker thought the farmer was going a bit far.

' ... doing our bit for the war effort,' Mr Epson carried, on ignoring Tucker, 'even when they send us *bad* kids ...' he looked at Tucker and his eyes went wide as if a thought had just occurred to him. '... for all we know, you might be an enemy spy!'

'Hey!' Tucker didn't like where this was going one bit.

'... no, I've made my mind up, we'll be writing to the War Office first thing tomorrow and sending you back to London. Until then, you'll be staying right here, where we can keep an eye on you!'

Tucker spent the rest of the day staring miserably out of the window in the farmer's kitchen as the sun burned across the sky, ran out of energy and sank down behind some trees. There was no chance of using the telescope because the farmer's wife or the farmer were on guard duty, watching him the whole time.

For supper he was given some bread and a lump of chewy meat, which he finished in ten seconds flat because he was starving, then the farmer announced he was going to bed and that Tucker would be locked in the spare room overnight. A policeman would be coming the next day to take him to London.

As soon as he was sure they'd gone to their own room, Tucker ran to the window.

He took the Time Machine Telescope out and put it up to his eye. He was about to give it a twist when he saw the bomb crater. Perhaps, thought Tucker, surprising himself by how brave he suddenly felt (probably because he'd already survived being bombed that day). I might go and take a quick look before I go.

The farmhouse was a small, low cottage and there was a convenient hedge right underneath Tucker's window.

He crawled out of the small window and dropped down, easily.

'Ow!' said Tucker, all the same, as sharp, twiggy bits stuck up his nose and into his ears. He stood up, just his head pocking out of the bush and checked if the coast was clear. Mr and Mrs Epsom were still fast asleep and the yard was quiet and a bit creepy in the silvery moonlight. Tucker crept out of his hiding place, then crept past a small shed with a sign on the top that said GODFREY THE GOAT, and where soft, goaty snoring noises came from within. Tucker tiptoed past, out of the yard and onto the track that led to the road.

So far, so good.

Unfortunately, he didn't notice the snoring

had stopped and a pair of beady-black eyes flicked open. They watched Tucker carefully.

But, by the time he was halfway down the track and away from the farm, his eyes had grown used to the dark and everything all around was almost as clear as if it was still daytime.

He only had to hop over the gate that led off the drive, and then go down a smaller track, where the slurry tower had recently been … before it been blown up by a lunatic. He'd never seen a real bomb crater before, and he wasn't going to miss the opportunity now.

Tucker's nose wrinkled as he got closer: the grass, the hedge, even trees were all dressed in muddy poo. And now he thought about it, it somehow seemed darker here: and the gloopy branches were stretched out like skeleton arms covered in gore. Tucker read horror stories whenever he could get his hands on them, but they weren't good for the imagination, especially when you're out at night all on your own.

Beginning to wonder if this was still such a good idea, he kept going but he tried not to look at the trees with their terrible claws and he breathed through his mouth to avoid the awful smell.

Worst of all, he had no idea that the farmer's goat, Godfrey, had sneaked out of its hut and was following him from the shadows.

A low wind moaned through the branches ... Tucker started to whistle 'woo, woo, toot toot' ... to keep his spirits up although it also helped anyone – especially goats – to know just where Tucker was, even in the darkness under the trees.

He arrived at the lip of the crater and peered curiously in. The moonlight shone down on the wreckage of the slurry tower, like some smashed rocket ship. The hole was HUGE.

Tucker bent down to get a better view of the pit, his eyes scanning the twisted metal, wondering if anything was left of the bomb. He was leaning over as far as he could, when something small, hairy and permanently angry (Godfrey the Goat) shot out from the trees and hit him very hard in the bottom.

For one glorious moment, Tucker knew what it was like to fly ... right before he found out what it was like to land in a poo pond.

'Bla, blech, urgh!' this was easily the worst thing that had ever happened to him. But Tucker didn't have any time to feel sorry for himself as his heard an evil goaty snicker and looked up to see Godfrey the Gruesome Goat throw himself down the slope.

It still wants to eat me, thought Tucker, even though I'm covered in poo, perhaps because I'm covered in poo – it's like gravy for goats – and I saw a programme once, they're really good at climbing.

Over the course of the next ten seconds, Tucker found he was a much faster runner than he had ever thought possible. Like a trained athlete, he leapt up from where he had landed and was out of the crater and halfway across the field when he heard a sort of strangled eurk! noise wasn't and realised he wasn't being chased anymore.

He stopped and turned. Godfrey now hung in the air, about three foot of the chain he must have broken wrapped around a tree root at the lip of the crater. Eurk, eurk! the goat said again, looking very sorry for himself.

'Good!' said Tucker, 'serves you right!' and he turned to go.

Then stopped.

He couldn't leave Godfrey hanging there – although it was stupid, as he'd probably chase him all over again … or worse – Tucker walked back to the crater.

'You promise not to eat me if I let you go?'

'Eurk!' said Godfrey, not very convincingly. But when Tucker unwrapped the chain, Godfrey, dropped a couple of feet to the ground, coughed and gave Tucker a sort of Sorry for Butting You look, before wobbling off into the night.

'Bye, bye Godfrey,' said Tucker. 'I'm not going to miss you.'

Then he took out his telescope and turned.

Chapter 8
Time Machine Tag

Tucker's return home was NOT a success. Unfortunately, his parents had got back before he thought they would. The reason was simple: they weren't used to shopping together and they'd had an argument about fishfingers v turkey dinosaurs in the middle of the supermarket and left.

This was why his mother opened the door as he walked up the path.

'Where have you been?' was the first thing she asked and, 'what's that terrible smell?' was the second.

'I, um,' Tucker was too tired and his bottom was too sore to think up a decent excuse. 'I was doing homework research and it went a bit wrong.'

'Well, we were worried sick!' said his mother. 'You can stay in your room for the rest of the day.'

'But have a shower first,' added his dad.

So, Tucker was grounded, for the second time that day and (for once) it wasn't his fault.

It was getting dark by the time he'd managed to wash all the poo out of his ears. Back in his bedroom, Tucker got into his pyjamas, sighed and went to close the curtains.

Outside the street was foggy: the dark shadows the street lights couldn't reach were like pools of black water that hid things.

Maybe he had gone too far bringing his parents back home? It felt weird – it might have seemed like a good idea but it wasn't what they were used to.

Perhaps he should change things back to the way they were? But that would be tricky – he was getting confused now with all this going back and forth and what if he just made things worse?

Tucker frowned and shivered as the swirling mist below got thicker and more ghostly. He went to close the curtain when something outside caught his eye.

Under one of the trees, half covered by fog he could see the dark shape of someone. Someone he'd seen before but about a million years into the future. Something about the way it stood there, head tilted up at Tucker's window, made him very sure that he was being watched. Even from underneath their hoodie.

With everything going on, Tucker suddenly didn't feel as brave as he had done at the farmer's house. Faced with a scary person outside his window, he did exactly what millions of kids all round the world would have done.

Tucker yanked the curtains shut, jumped into bed and pulled the covers over his head.

If I ignore it, it will go away he thought.

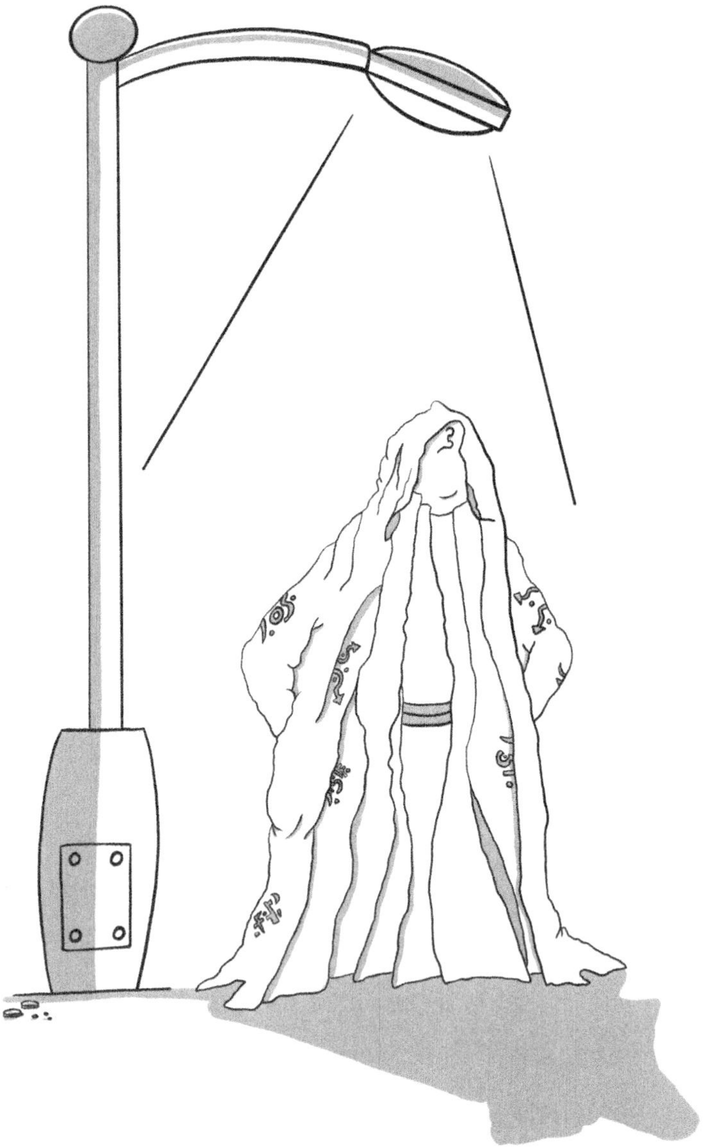

But it was a long, slow night.

Tucker must have drifted off at some point because when he woke, it was to the sound of rain hammering on his window. He got up and looked outside. The sky was a murky grey, like old dishwater and it looked like it was going to rain all day. He peered up and down the street, squinting through the sheets of rain and eventually breathed a sigh of relief. At least the frightening follower underneath the tree across the street had gone.

However, Tucker still felt uneasy as he went down to breakfast. Whoever it was must have been following him since the start. He remembered seeing him across the Thames in Tudor times. Perhaps he'd been in the jungle, too but Tucker hadn't noticed thanks to all the giant spiders and dinosaurs. But why was he following him? His toast stuck to the roof of his dry mouth. He pushed his plate away but neither of his parents said anything about wasting food: his mum looked almost as cross as she had been the night before and his dad seemed ... well, unhappy.

And it was all his doing.

Tucker looked at them both and made a BIG decision, right then and there. He got up.

'Can I be excused from the table, mum?' His mother looked up.

'Ye'es,' she said a little uncertainly. 'But you've hardly touched your food.'

'Don't worry, I'll come back and finish it very soon, right now I've got to be somewhere else.'

'Where's that?' his dad looked just as confused as his mum.

'Last Tuesday!' said Tucker over his shoulder as he ran out the front door.

He ran all the way to the workman's hole where he had originally found the Time Machine Telescope. Then he reached into his inside pocket and pulled it out. As he put it to his eye he didn't notice the person in a black hoodie across the road. Instead, he thought about his mum and dad. 'I'm going to make things got back to the way they were before ...,' he said out loud. He would even put the Telescope back, get attacked by Kylo Hen and spend the day with Mrs Dempsey. It was a pity about the scope but everything else would be better.

Then he turned the dial as he counted the days back with the rise and fall of the sun.

When Tucker took the Telescope away from his eye, he was expecting it to be just a few days earlier.

Instead, it was broad daylight and sunny… and Medieval? Something had gone wrong. Tucker scratched his head and looked about. He was standing in the middle of a road of sorts, except it was mainly just dust and dirt. The neat, terraced houses that he had been expecting were gone, to be replaced by thatched cottages and fields with people working in them using their bare hands or simple tools. The air smelled fresh and he could hear birdsong – it was quite nice, but *definitely* not where Tucker needed to be.

He was looking at the telescope, wondering what had happened when he heard the sound of young voices. He looked up to see a group of children over the road. Tucker was so surprised and pleased to see kids he shouted, 'Hello!' and waved.

He was only vaguely aware of the sudden sound of large horse's hooves behind him as he did, because a large kid with a runny nose had just thrown a turnip at him.

Which is why Tucker ducked, which is why whoever it was on the horse who was thundering towards him, got hit in the face with a large vegetable.

'Oof!' said the cloaked figure on the horse, as Tucker straightened up, just in time to recognise it was the same cloaked figure who had been outside his window last night, now galloping past, scattering the kids, including Snotty Turnip

Thrower.

Who fell in a pond.

Making a mental note to stop waving at people, Tucker grabbed the telescope as the giant horse and its cloaked rider turned towards him.

Twist ... bang, music, lights etc

Tucker had already been to the future before but not like this.

London had been replaced by a huge, rainbow sea. The strange, brightly-coloured water surrounded the small island he was standing on, with waves of green, orange and gold rolling towards him, their crests capped with sparkling silver foam. It was the most beautiful thing Tucker had ever seen and he was wondering what time he was in when he saw something sticking out of the water about a hundred feet away. It looked like the end of a snorkel.

Tucker watched closely as it moved towards him and started to come out of the water, just as a huge shadow, suggesting something very large underneath, appeared beneath it.

Tucker's mouth dropped as an enormous shark burst out of the colourful waves.

And it was being ridden by the mysterious cloaked figure.

How's he keep following me?! Tucker just had time to think before the snorkel on top of the shark's head swivelled in his direction and shot out a net.

Twist!

He was standing in a long room, lined with golden mirrors, beautiful paintings and small tables covered with little pink cakes. Someone in the corner was playing a harp, whilst someone else was playing what looked like a small piano that made a quite-attractive twangy sound.

Everyone else was staring at Tucker.

'Bertie!' said a man in a tall white wig and a red coat. 'There appears to be a street beggar in your drawing room.'

'So there does!' said another man in an even bigger wig who Tucker assumed was Bertie. 'And he's eating my cake.'

'Sorry,' said Tucker, 'I'm absolutely starving. These are delicious, by the way.'

Bertie looked very like he had something to say about that but his attention (and everyone else's) was grabbed when a lady in the room screamed.

'There's a terrifying figure at the window! Oh, I think I'm going to faint!'

'And he looks like he's trying to get in.'

'Who is it?' someone else demanded to know.

'Aargh!' said Tucker, because that's the only thing you can say, really, when a cloaked figure you last saw on a giant robot shark a million years in the future was now perching on a window ledge in the 18th Century. He couldn't believe that his scary and mysterious follower had found him so fast but he needed to slow him down. 'I think he's a Frenchman!' Tucker shouted and watched as several English noblemen and ladies ran towards the cloaked figure at the window who panicked and fell backwards into a hedge.

Twist!!

Luckily Tucker had his eyes open for once, because he was now standing at the foot of a volcano and a river of lava was oozing towards him.

Tucker turned to run but a whistling sound made him look up.

A meteorite was coming towards him and – although he couldn't be sure – there was a cloaked figure perched on its top …

Twist!!!

Snow.

Snow up.

Snow down.

Snow falling from a white, snowy sky.

After the intense heat of the volcano, it was almost a relief. Until his entire body went numb with cold.

In fact, the chattering sound of his teeth nearly covered up the whirring sound above his head.

Tucker looked up at the giant airship as it came out of the sky like a floating whale. It was trailing a long banner.

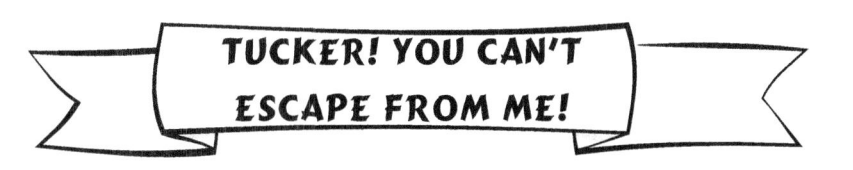

> **TUCKER! YOU CAN'T ESCAPE FROM ME!**

said the banner.

Tucker threw a snowball at it.

Twist!!!!

In this time, Tucker was on top of huge tower. All about him a storm raged, with thunder, howling winds and flashes of lightning that lit up a landscape crawling with strange creatures: feathered tigers, fire breathing lions … a unicorn with a snake for a tail flashed past the top of the tower, its powerful wings beating through the driving rain.

It felt like the past, but some different time, a past that might never have happened, except in someone's imagination. I'm in the time of myth and magic, realised Tucker.

A tunnel of flame seared across the night sky as a dragon burst from swirling clouds. And Tucker just knew who would be riding it.

He was about to twist again when a bolt of lightning struck the tower.

Tucker fell.

This time he didn't twist.

He couldn't.

He hardly had time to pull the scope from his pocket as he felt himself tumbling through the dark.

He heard the dragon roar, half a roll of thunder ... and then silence.

In an instant, the air felt warmer and Tucker was no longer falling through the eye of the storm.

Instead, he was falling a much shorter distance through a hedge, by a pavement.

Tucker landed on his side with a loud 'oof!'

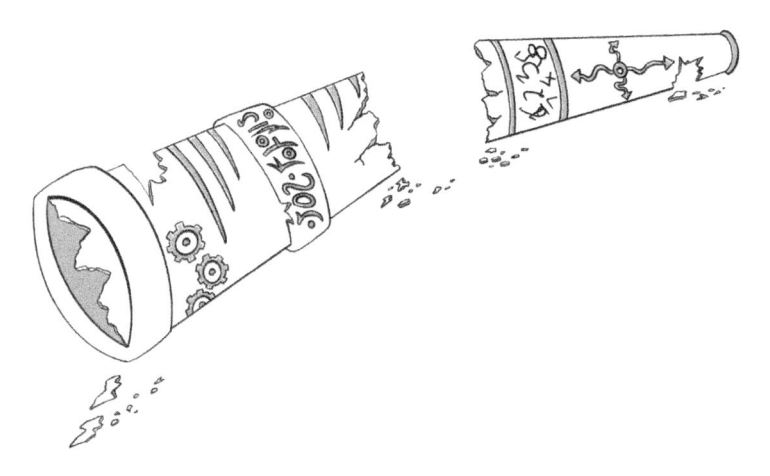

and looked about. He was back in his own time, lying next to the workman's hole.

Something tinkled when he sat up, bits of metal dropping on the concrete and Tucker suddenly had a very bad feeling indeed.

He looked down and saw the broken pieces of the Time Machine Telescope. He'd landed on it when he'd fallen, and, as the meaning of what the broken telescope meant sank in, Tucker felt like crying.

He'd messed everything up – as usual.

But this time it was much, much worse. He hadn't just broken his bike or smashed a plate. He probably broken Time itself and he'd definitely broken the only thing that would be able to put everything right, like he'd promised.

He was in deep, deep trouble.

Tucker put his head in his hands and was concentrating so hard on taking long breaths (in between groaning miserably), he didn't notice the figure in dark robes and a hood walking towards him until whoever it was put a hand on his shoulder.

Chapter 9
Time before Time

'At last,' said the robed figure. Tucker raised his head to looked at the face that was peering with concern into his.

And his brain did a sort of cartwheel, then it did a few backflips and a little mad dance for good measure.

'Tucker???' he gasped. The (very familiar) face grinned back.

'Yup, that's right – I am you, but another you,' he said. Tucker looked closely at the slightly older version of himself. He guessed he must be about sixteen: a bit taller, hair a bit longer but the most obvious difference was the eyepatch.

'How did I ... er, do that to your eye?'

Other Tucker looked a bit confused for half a second, then lifted the patch up. The eye underneath twinkled back at him.

'I didn't, it's my way of travelling through time, but I can keep one eye on the present day, which can be useful. It's just a replacement to the telescope ... that you broke, by the way.'

'I know. I'm really, *really* sorry.'

'Don't worry about that – right now we probably should go somewhere else before that policeman over there starts asking us questions.'

Tucker looked around and saw that there was, indeed, a policeman giving suspicious looks at the two identical twins of different ages, one dressed like a large bat.

Tucker Two, grabbed Tucker One's shoulder firmly. 'Hold on!' he said.

And the world went black.

Then, just like that, they were standing in a room.

It was warm and quiet but nothing like any other place he'd ever seen in his life. For this room floated in space. Its walls were made of clear glass, so that Tucker could see on one side there was pure, absolute darkness – more black and deeper than he ever thought possible. And the other side, the Universe was even more dramatic: exploding outwards, like every firework in the Cosmos going off at the same time ... over and over again.

'Cor!' said Tucker. But that didn't really cover it.

'Pretty impressive, eh?' said Tucker Two. 'Those are stars being born ... and, on the other side is the Time Before Time Itself.'

'So where are we?'

'London still, I suppose – as usual, the main question is *when* are we? ... and the answer to that is we're balancing right on the edge of time. I've never had guests before, so sorry for the mess.'

Tucker dragged his eyes away from the huge events going on outside and looked around the room. It was furnished with comfy sofas and leather armchairs, of the sort that came with large velvet cushions and, scattered everywhere, were treasures from every place and every age:

suits of armour, gold plates, laser guns, tribal spears, space helmets, oil paintings, a cricket bat, and lots of complicated maps. It looked like a cross between a wizard's sitting room, a pirate's den and a toy shop. He pointed at something hanging from a beam.

'What's that?'

'Ah, the Friendship Rope. Put that around an enemy's wrist or any other part of their body and they'll instantly become your best friend. Doesn't work on dragons and those yappy small dogs that belong to old ladies for some reason.'

'Still cool ... and is that...?'

'The Time Machine Telescope? Yes.'

'But I thought I'd broken it.'

'You broke the one in your time, but this is one from another time – two can exist at once, like you and I are standing here now.'

'It's all a bit complicated.'

'Yes,' admitted Tucker Two. 'And I don't really understand a lot of it myself. All I know for sure is that time travel works and it's great fun. When

I discovered you had the Telescope, I started watching you. Then I got worried you might do something stupid and I tried to make contact and explain some important things. But you kept running away.'

'Sorry.'

'Don't be, those were some pretty cool moves.'

'Thanks. What did you want to tell me?'

'Loads, but the main thing is that you've got an important job to do.' Tucker One looked at Tucker two.

'Oh, yeah, what's that?'

'Well,' Tucker Two stared hard back at him. 'As well as being irresponsible and a bit annoying you're also a Multidimensional Agent. In fact you, Tucker, are the youngest member of The Noble Company of Time Radicals.'

'Who are they?'

'They … *you* stop other time travellers from messing things up. You see, it's not just the Time Machine Telescope, there are loads of important artifacts and objects all over the Galaxy that allow people to slip through time or they might have other powers, like the Friendship Rope. In the wrong hands, they could cause all sorts of disasters.'

'Where did all these objects come from?'

'Aliens.'

'Aliens?'

'Yup.'

'Sick!' Tucker found he had another question. 'How come me … or you?'

'I'm still trying to figure that out. All I know is that, sooner or later you were destined to find the Telescope. But, also, to most people, it would just be an ordinary tube that lets you look at things from far away. It didn't even work that well for me, when I found it. You're a natural Time Radical, perhaps the best I've ever seen. I can't work out if you're amazing or just really, really lucky.'

'Lucky?! Since this whole thing has started, I've been attacked by a chicken, nearly run over by a horse ... twice, butted in the bottom by a goat and someone I've never met tried to drop a bomb on me!'

'Yeah, but you're still here. You're only just starting out Tucker – you've got a fantastic future ahead of you. And past!'

'But if I broke my telescope, that's it, isn't it? I won't be able to put things back – I never should have changed things just so my parents came home and I didn't have to be dealing with mad chickens on my own.'

'I can help there.'

'Really?'

'Yes. But the main thing is you realised our parents are needed elsewhere, right now, doing important jobs. And you realised that on your own. And you also probably don't need me to tell you you're still the most important thing to them and they'll always be there for you. They proved that by coming back when you asked them to.'

'I guess,' said Tucker One. 'Thanks for pointing that out, anyway.'

'Don't mention it.'

'I actually don't mind them being away so much,' Tucker One said. 'It's amazing how hard it is to get away with stuff when they're home all the time. I guess all families work differently.'

'Yup! But, seriously, don't worry too much about that stuff,' said Tucker Two, smiling kindly. 'It took me a long time to learn that you can only change the small things – and then only a bit. Concentrate on our mission and on enjoying yourself, instead, it's a great gift.' Tucker Two suddenly stopped.

'You know, it's just occurred to me, perhaps this was all meant to be, and you were meant to meet me? Anyway, you've got stuff to do at home and then an important job saving the universe, so, before you go, you can choose one thing – except my Telescope, of course.'

Tucker looked about to be polite, but he knew immediately what he really wanted. He pointed at it and wiggled his eyebrows hopefully.

'Of course,' Tucker Two grinned. 'And now I

think I can make things right.'

Tucker felt relief running through him like sunlight.

'How?'

By way of an answer, the older boy flicked his eyepatch down and held onto Tucker's shoulder once again.

'Like this.'

Chapter 10
... and we're back to Chickens

Thomas Tucker (or just *Tucker* to everyone who knew him) was walking innocently down the street near his home. Just minding his own business.

He was on his way to the Mrs Dempsey, the lady who looked after him in the holidays. His parents often worked until very late – but that was OK, they always had a great time at the weekend or when they went on holiday.

This was going to be the most important day of Tucker's life, and he knew it – because just around the corner, in a hole, was a marvellous object of great power.

But, first, he had an important date to keep.

The sun was warm on his face, and it made him scrunch his eyes up, so he heard the chicken before he saw it.

'Cluck,' went the chicken.

Ah! thought Tucker forcing his eyes open: he knew that cluck.

Kylo Hen.

A small chicken with black and red feathers was standing right there, right in the middle of the pavement. Tucker's arch enemy glared at Tucker with one terrible beady eye, then its head made a slightly bonkers, jerky movement.

'We meet again,' said Tucker, reaching into his sleeve.

'Cluck!' agreed Kylo Hen scratching the ground and there was the sound of a tree splintering behind him. But Tucker was already moving, the Friendship Rope lassoing out of his hands. There was a flutter of feathers, the throwing of a rope and a very surprised squawk!

Much later that day, Tucker's parents arrived home – both at the same time.

'Hi, Mum, hi, Dad!' he shouted from his bedroom. 'Be down in a sec!'

He shoved the Time Machine Telescope to the back of the wardrobe and bounded downstairs three at a time. His mother was putting her bag on the kitchen table and staring out of the window.

'Tucker, is that a chicken in the garden? It looks scary.'

'Yes, that's Kylo Hen. And she's actually very friendly – once you get to know her.' The Friendship rope had worked brilliantly, even after he had taken it off.

His dad came in and gave them both a hug. 'What's for supper, I'm starving?' He looked out of the window. 'Chicken?'

'Dad!'

'Alright, shall we order a takeaway instead?

Anything you like.'

Tucker smiled, things were really back to normal at home.

Then he looked at the note he had found on his bed.

Your training starts now!

THE NOBLE ORDER OF TIME RADICALS

... and tomorrow would be the start of the greatest adventure of his life.

Just the Beginning

Robin Bennett

When Robin grew up, he thought he wanted to be a soldier until everyone else realised that putting him in charge of a tank was a very bad idea. He then became an assistant gravedigger in London. After that he had a career frantically starting businesses (everything from dog-sitting to cigars, tuition to translation)... until finally settling down to write improbable stories to keep his children from killing each other on long car journeys.

Matt Cherry

Matt grew up on the Kent coast, writing and drawing, where he still lives today. He still loves to write and draw, so he hasn't changed much really. He's just a lot taller.

Matt is the author of The Monster Spotter's Handbook Vol 1 and 2 and has illustrated the Stupendous Sports series by Robin Bennett.

Printed in Great Britain
by Amazon